How to Use This Book

There are several different ways you may want to use this book.

- Read the pages straight through, in order, and hear the contributors speak about these four themes:

    Seeking Spiritual Understanding
    Living Together on This Small Planet
    Co-Creating with the Divine
    Focusing on What Is Most Important in Life

- Dip in and out, perhaps finding your favorite contributors' insights first, and discover the rich nuggets of wisdom from the other contributors along the way.

- Take it like a daily vitamin supplement—and focus on the health your body and soul can glean from it.

- Read it with a friend.

- Use it for group study. Focus first on the self-tests to get to know each other; then talk together about the contributors' ideas, and yours.

To jump-start your spiritual life, you might want to take ten days to explore each of the four themes in the book. Over this period of forty days—a period of time traditionally associated with mindful preparation—rely on the help offered here. Then, set your own course and take new steps on your own path.

Forty Days to Begin a Spiritual Life

Today's Most Inspiring Teachers Help You on Your Way

Maura Shaw and the Editors at SkyLight Paths

Foreword by Dan Wakefield,
author of *Releasing the Creative Spirit*

Walking Together, Finding the Way
SKYLIGHT PATHS Publishing
Nashville, Tennessee

Forty Days to Begin a Spiritual Life:
Today's Most Inspiring Teachers Help You on Your Way

Library of Congress Cataloging-in-Publication Data

Forty days to begin a spiritual life / [compiled by] Maura Shaw and the editors at SkyLight Paths.
       p.   cm.
Includes bibliographical references.
ISBN 1-893361-48-9 (pbk.)
1. Spiritual life. I. Shaw, Maura. II. SkyLight Paths Publishing.
BL624 .F664 2002
291.4'4—dc21

2001057811

10 9 8 7 6 5 4 3 2

Walking Together, Finding the Way
Published by SkyLight Paths Publishing
A Division of LongHill Partners, Inc.
An Imprint of Turner Publishing Company
4507 Charlotte Avenue, Suite 100
Nashville, TN 37209
Tel: (615) 255-2665
www.skylightpaths.com

SkyLight Paths Publishing is pleased to donate
the royalties from this book to Habitat for
Humanity and the Make-A-Wish® Foundation
in the names of the contributors:

Karen Armstrong
Sylvia Boorstein
Frederic and Mary Ann Brussat
Rabbi David A. Cooper
Br. Victor-Antoine d'Avila-Latourrette
Mitch Finley
Dr. Eugene Fisher
Tamar Frankiel
Matthew Gilbert
Fr. Joseph F. Girzone
Judy Greenfeld
Rev. Theodore M. Hesburgh, CSC
Rodger Kamenetz
Lawrence Kushner
Patrick Marrin
Katherine Paterson
Fr. M. Basil Pennington, OCSO
Sandy Eisenberg Sasso
Kathy Shaidle
Dr. Bernie Siegel
Rt. Rev. Krister Stendahl
Phyllis Tickle
Rabbi Arthur Waskow
Dr. Andrew Weil
Jane Yolen

"Each one of us is in the process of spiritual growth from the moment we are born until death and beyond," writes Sylvia Boorstein, one of many wise voices heard in this book. If we take her at her word—and I do—this means you are in that process right now. You were before and you will be during and after reading this book—and, I hope, not just reading but also participating in these pages. You have that opportunity, not only as reader but as writer, for there are spaces provided to respond with your own reactions and insights and thoughts to this wide-ranging array of teachers and guides from around the world, from a world of different spiritual paths, all with a similar aim: to come awake.

Words may waken you, may jolt you like thunder, soothe you like sunsets, show you a way—show you that perhaps you are already on it and now may enjoy and find fulfillment on the path you have taken, are taking, will take. Here in these pages record your own steps, trace your own map (which was already there), become aware of the guideposts and street signs designed from others' experience. Follow or ignore or simply take note of these signs and lights, and create your own. Waken to your own resources, gifts and possibilities, as various as those of the men and women whose words are offered here.

"Spirit," defines the *Oxford English Dictionary*, is "the animating or vital principle in [humans] (and animals); that which gives life to the physical organism, in contrast to its purely material elements; the breath of life."

You have it!

Like the "would-be gentleman" of Molière's comedy *Le bourgeois gentilhomme* who didn't know he'd been speaking "prose," we are rightly thrilled to discover, or remember (for we all forget), that we are spiritual beings. The words within this book will not only remind us of that blessed reality but reinforce our awareness of it, enlarging and enlivening our appreciation of who and what we are and may yet be.

—**Dan Wakefield**
author of *Releasing the Creative Spirit:*
Unleash the Creativity in Your Life

Forty Days to Begin a Spiritual Life

What Does It Mean to Begin a Spiritual Life?

AT CERTAIN TIMES in our lives we stand at the threshold of something new—marriage, parenthood, college, a new career—and, for most of us, getting to that point required preparation, even dedication and hard work. Our new way of life most likely began with a desire and evolved into a plan. Along the way we consulted experts, teachers, friends—anyone who could give us helpful tips and an insider's advice on the new world we were about to enter.

Beginning a spiritual life is no different. We start with a time of preparation, a willingness to accept advice and counsel from wise teachers, and eventually we arrive at a place where spiritual meaning is present in our life every day. In taking time outside of the normal course to reflect on our spirituality, we are following in the footsteps of Moses, Jesus, Buddha and Muhammad. However, the path we choose will be ours alone, discovered through self-examination, reflection and spiritual transformation.

To help you get started, the editors at SkyLight Paths have created a resource in which some of the most respected spiritual teachers in America—teachers from all faiths and spiritual traditions—share their personal spiritual priorities with you. We hope that you will use this book in such a way that, years from now, you will see it as one of the signposts that helped you: first, to become aware of where you were spiritually and, then, to move further along your spiritual path.

Why did we call this book *Forty Days to Begin a Spiritual Life*? As Rabbi David A. Cooper says, "There is magic in the number forty: Moses on the mountain, Jesus in the desert, Elijah in the cave, the Hebrews in the wilderness, the days of rain in the Flood of Noah" (*Three Gates to Meditation Practice: A Personal Journey into Sufism, Buddhism, and Judaism* [SkyLight Paths, 2000], p. 23). In many religious traditions, spiritual leaders began their active ministries after a retreat spent in contemplation, prayer and fasting. This time of preparation often occupied the space of forty days, a time that appears to have a special resonance in the human soul and in the Divine order.

Do we need to spend forty days to take inventory of our spiritual lives? Of course not. But the echo of the phrase "forty days" can resound in our hearts, moving us toward transformation on our unique spiritual paths. How much time you devote to finding your way is up to you. Just as we invited spiritual teachers and authors of all faiths to share their personal spiritual priorities, this pathway-in-book-format invites *you* to examine the priorities of your life.

Some of our contributors' comments will surprise or enlighten you. All of them are beautiful, brief representations of what they teach about or write about, what they do in the world. Our hope is that you will use this selection of very practical advice to help direct and redirect yourself, to help change your life in ways that are spiritually meaningful.

We also asked these twenty-three spiritual leaders to share one image, story or allegory that encapsulates our common spiritual quest. The result is a fascinating array of images of our spiritual lives: Holy Envy, the Labyrinth, the Well, Pilgrim People, the Hero's Journey. Plus, you will find brief stories from Karen Armstrong, Lawrence Kushner, Tamar Frankiel and Judy Greenfeld, and Jane Yolen. Their stories may give you some of the words you need to write down your own stories. It is often in the stories of our lives that we find God.

Surrounding each contributor's insights are three more things to help you shape your spiritual self:

- Brief descriptions of interesting religious traditions and tales, under the heading "Did You Know?"

- Samplings of prayers, texts or quotes from religious traditions and spiritual leaders of the past, under the heading "Every Life Is a Spiritual Conversation with the Divine."

- Hands-on suggestions for your spiritual practice, under the heading "A Spiritual Practice to Help You on Your Way."

Each of us has the ability to jump-start a spiritual life, but no one can do it for you. What we can do for you, with the resource you hold in your hands, is to offer tools you can use to take your spiritual temperature and to look as if through a wide-view lens at your life, in order to take charge of where you are heading, and where you want to be going, in your spiritual and religious life. We hope you find yourself refreshed, renewed and inspired.

How to Use This Book

There are several different ways you may want to use this book.

- Read the pages straight through, in order, and hear the contributors speak about these four themes:

  Seeking Spiritual Understanding
  Living Together on This Small Planet
  Co-Creating with the Divine
  Focusing on What Is Most Important in Life

- Dip in and out, perhaps finding your favorite contributors' insights first, and discover the rich nuggets of wisdom from the other contributors along the way.

- Take it like a daily vitamin supplement—and focus on the health your body and soul can glean from it.

- Read it with a friend.

- Use it for group study. Focus first on the self-tests to get to know each other; then talk together about the contributors' ideas, and yours.

To jump-start your spiritual life, you might want to take ten days to explore each of the four themes in the book. Over this period of forty days—a period of time traditionally associated with mindful preparation—rely on the help offered here. Then, set your own course and take new steps on your own path.

Seeking Spiritual Understanding

Seeking Spiritual Understanding

66 *S*| *piritual maturity is not something to get,*
rather it is something we already have within us."

—Rabbi David A. Cooper (see page 22)

Where Do We Find Spiritual Understanding?

WE FIND SPIRITUAL UNDERSTANDING in many ways and through many practices—study, prayer, meditation and worship among them. We find spiritual understanding in many places—church, synagogue, temple, ashram, monastery, half-way house, kitchen table and retreat center among them. Most of all, we find spiritual understanding in ourselves. No one can give it to you, sell it to you or bestow it on you. Even when we gain spiritual understanding within a particular faith tradition, the understanding is uniquely ours. We are each unique, with enormous possibilities. As Walt Whitman said, "I contain multitudes."

You are on a spiritual path at once similar to all of us and simultaneously your own. Just the fact that you have picked up this book shows that you are seeking to improve, change or simply deepen your life with the Divine Mystery. This can often happen within a faith tradition through its scriptures, teachers and community of believers. Other times a book is just what we need to animate our spiritual lives and point us in the right direction.

Use the writings and ideas in this section as a map for finding the source—or several sources—for your spiritual growth. We all have a relationship with God, a path of enlightenment, a spiritual walk. Understanding that path's starting point, its reason for being, can help us to understand and become more aware of the spirituality that exists at *every* point along the path. Sometimes good advice—someone else's ideas and practices—provides just what we need to stimulate spiritual understanding.

How Does Good Advice Become Spiritual Understanding?

We must move beyond simply hearing good ideas to incorporating them into our lives. Throughout this book are sections called "A Spiritual Practice to Help You on Your Way." These are proven spiritual practices of various religious traditions designed to help you translate great ideas into meaningful practice. These will help you turn good advice into spiritual understanding.

Take this self-test with one or more other people. Choose people you trust, people you want to know better and whom you want to know you better.

Answer each question 'True' or 'False.'

1. I want people to know that I have a spiritual life.   TRUE   FALSE
2. I have recently had a spiritual insight or experience.   TRUE   FALSE
3. I gain spiritual insight through reading, praying, studying or talking to other people.   TRUE   FALSE
4. I think my experience of the sacred is unique.   TRUE   FALSE
5. Certain religious practices are vital to my spiritual life.   TRUE   FALSE

Talk about each question and why you answered "True" or "False." There are no right or wrong answers. Above all, be honest with yourself.

Do you wish any of your answers were different? If so, why? Are any of your answers different at this point on your path than they were at an earlier time in your life? Noticing differences often helps us to see our own spirituality in a clearer way.

Rabbi David A. Cooper, author of *God Is a Verb;*
A Heart of Stillness: A Complete Guide to Learning
the Art of Meditation; and *Three Gates to Meditation*
Practice: A Personal Journey into Sufism, Buddhism,
and Judaism

"One of my personal, spiritual priorities
for the future is . . .

To re-establish a healthy relationship between the teachings that flow
through me and the person doing the teaching. Thus, my personal priorities will involve generally slowing down, paring away some activities altogether, being less immediately responsive to the demands of instant
communication, paying less attention to the continuous flow of media,
and thereby having more awareness of the richness of each moment while
I extend and sustain periods of paying attention to the mysterious
unfolding of the constant continuum called NOW."

—Rabbi David A. Cooper

Did You Know?

The ascetics of many faith traditions have focused their spiritual practice on renouncing the body, in favor of a life of the
spirit. The desert monks of the Christian tradition (5th–7th
centuries), for instance, called the body a "tomb" and a
"prison." In contrast, most spiritual teachers today emphasize
the ways in which our spirituality can be "embodied," and our
bodies can help us toward spiritual understanding.

"One image or allegory that encapsulates our common spiritual quest is . . .

When a frog is dropped into a pan of boiling water, naturally, it jumps right out. However, if the frog is put into water that has only a very low flame under it, the frog will often sit quietly without realizing the water is slowly heating until it is too late. Each of us has a natural inclination to 'save' ourselves from the boiling waters of everyday distractions and material seductions. Our souls yearn to realize and experience connections with the source of being. Combined, these yearnings add up to the common goal of attaining a new level of consciousness in which everything looks different than the way it appears now. In Kabbalah, this is referred to as messianic consciousness, an awareness of the interconnectedness of all things. Thus, our task is to realize where we are. If we fall asleep, we can only pray that someone will awaken us before we are cooked. If we stay alert, we are able to notice others who may be cooking slowly, and we do whatever we can to remind them—and ourselves—of the common destiny of human consciousness."

—Rabbi David A. Cooper

Every life is a spiritual conversation with the Divine.
(Space here for reflection.)

The rich will make temples for Siva:
What shall I, a poor man, do?
My legs are pillars, the body is a shrine,
The head is the cupola, of gold.

—Basava, a Hindu
reformer (12th century)

"One *spiritual insight that I would like to share with others as they think about their priorities on their path to a rewarding spiritual life is . . .*

A teaching that I always use when working with meditators on retreat: If we stop at any point during our day and pay complete attention to the physical experience of one breath or one step, we are able to fully engage our awareness for that brief period of time. You can try this right now. Stop reading for the next breath, close your eyes, and experience the total body movement around the breath.... Now, if you have taken one breath with total concentration, ask yourself what the difference is between the complete awareness you just had and the awareness of a fully enlightened being who notices her or his breath? The truth is that there is no difference. Awareness is awareness. When we are able to integrate this understanding, and realize that we innately have the potential for complete awareness, we gain the insight that our spiritual maturity is not something to get, rather it is something we already have within us. The task, of course, is to learn how to gain stability from one breath to the next without being distracted, and this is quite demanding. But anytime we remember, we simply take the next breath or the next step in its fullness, and this brings us continually closer to the extraordinary potential that rests within."

—Rabbi David A. Cooper

A Spiritual Practice to Help You on Your Way

As Rabbi Cooper suggests above: Take time now to pay complete attention to your breathing. Set aside the next two minutes—120 seconds—to focus on this physical activity. (If you have a difficult time taking even two minutes "off" and simply focusing, setting a timer may help you to allow yourself to relax and release your mind from the activity around you.) Concentrate completely on only your breathing—going out, coming in. Remember the feeling of self-mastery this experience gives you, and return to it whenever you find yourself wandering.

Matthew Gilbert, former executive editor of *NAPRA ReView* and author of *Take This Job & Love It*

"**O**ne of my personal, spiritual priorities for the future is . . .

To bring a more vital sense of the sacred back into my everyday life. I have come to realize that while I do have strong spiritual beliefs and values, they don't always find their way into my daily activities, which I think is the point of being here on this planet living our spirituality all of the time, whether walking in nature or having a conversation or buying groceries for the week. For me it is like a muscle to be exercised; the more I do it, the easier it will become."

—Matthew Gilbert

Did You Know?

Sometimes the truth remains hidden until shown to us by a bold non-conformist or societal outcast sometimes called a "holy fool" or "holy idiot" in religious literature. Such a person can enrich our understanding in startling ways by example. Holy fools are common in the faith traditions of Russian Orthodoxy, Sufism and Zen Buddhism; they are often mystical teachers or hermits.

"One image or allegory that encapsulates our common spiritual quest is . . .

The hero's journey. We become heroes if we successfully overcome the obstacles of the small self in reaching a fuller realization of who we are as spiritual beings and as human beings. It's not a journey that takes us to a solitary mountaintop, but one that brings us more intimately into relationship with everything and everyone around us. We may never really know how far along we are on the path, and we will sometimes forget where we are going, but the true heroes will instinctually stay the course if they travel it with honor, integrity and intention."

—Matthew Gilbert

Every life is a spiritual conversation with the Divine.

(Space here for reflection.)

There is in all visible things an invisible fecundity, a dimmed light, a meek namelessness, a hidden wholeness.

—Thomas Merton, from his poem "Hagia Sophia"[i]

"One spiritual insight that I would like to share with others as they think about their priorities on their path to a rewarding spiritual life is . . .

There is no right path to enlightenment; there is only what we intuitively and humbly experience as truth for ourselves. As long as we respect others, as long as we are compassionate, sensitive and loving, and as long as we honor our own journey we will find our way. I truly believe that at the conclusion of this grand experience in humanness, no matter how many millennia it may take, we will all end up in the same place."

—Matthew Gilbert

A Spiritual Practice to Help You on Your Way

To be able to reach "a fuller realization of who we are" spiritually starts with identifying needs—*your needs,* which may include more silence, improved spiritual practice, study and so on; and *our common needs* for a better world, needs like peace, justice and an end to hunger. Take time now to write a list of needs. Looking over your list, decide what it says about your personal, spiritual goals.

Karen Armstrong, author of *A History of God* and *Islam: A Short History*

"One of my personal, spiritual priorities for the future is . . .

To become more acquainted with the spirituality and history of the non-theistic religions, such as Buddhism, which, I believe, have much to teach monotheists."

—Karen Armstrong

Did You Know?

Worship in eastern religious traditions takes many forms that are different from traditional western worship of God. In Hinduism, attending to God's enjoyment or entertainment is a popular form of *puja* ("worship" in Sanskrit). Jainist worship often involves offering food to a god. Buddhists often offer flowers to the Buddha in worship.

"One image or allegory that encapsulates our common spiritual quest is . . .

A story of Rabbi Hillel, who, when asked to recite the Torah while he stood on one leg, replied: 'Do not do unto others as you would not have done unto you: that is the Torah—go and learn it!'"

—Karen Armstrong

Every life is a spiritual conversation with the Divine.

(Space here for reflection.)

The way is like an empty vessel that we may still draw from.

—Lao Tzu, 6th century B.C.E., from *Tao Te Ching* (paraphrased)

66 **O** *ne spiritual insight that I would like to share with others as they think about their priorities on their path to a rewarding spiritual life is . . .*

Instead of becoming anxious about the existence of God, the discipline of compassion will bring us that ecstasy (transcendence of the self) and will give us a true experience of the sacred, however we define it."

—Karen Armstrong

A Spiritual Practice to Help You on Your Way

A tale is told of the Baal Shem Tov, the founder of Hasidism in the 18th century, that when he traveled alone on spiritual retreat, he would bring several loaves of bread and at the end of the week they would still be in his sack, to his great surprise. (See Martin Buber, *Tales of the Hasidim*, I, 45.) For the next week, de-emphasize preparing and eating food to enhance your concentration on matters of spiritual practice. Eat simply, and spend the saved time meditating, reviewing your self-test results, writing down your prayers, or doing some other spiritual practice that is important to you.

Jane Yolen, author of *Owl Moon,*
Milk & Honey and 200 other books

"One of my personal, spiritual priorities
for the future is . . .
To try and seek out the good in other people, rather than respond to
what I consider their misguided notions."

—Jane Yolen

Did You Know?

Many spiritual traditions teach that the Divine may be wor-
shiped in more than one way. Jesus taught his followers, "In
my house are many mansions." In Egyptian and Hindu traditions, gods often change form from morning to noon to
evening.

"One image or allegory that encapsulates our common spiritual quest is . . .

A story: A man leaves his wife and family to go on the road seeking truth. Only when he finally finds her, she is an old, wizened woman with lank gray hair and hardly a tooth in her head. Still she speaks in a low, beautiful voice, which is how he knows he has found her. After staying with her for a year and learning what she has to teach, he leaves. But first he asks if there is anything he can do for her. 'Yes,' she says. 'When you speak of me, tell them I am young and beautiful.'"

—Jane Yolen

Every life is a spiritual conversation with the Divine.

(Space here for reflection.)

As you give up yourself, in greater measure, God will fill you. Your essence becomes your holiness. In this way, God may become great in you.

—Meister Eckhart, early 14th-century German Christian mystic, *Talks of Instruction,* 4–5 (paraphrased)

"One spiritual insight that I would like to share with others as they think about their priorities on their path to a rewarding spiritual life is . . .

Truth is old, but we see her as new, reclothing her in our own clothes and makeup."

—Jane Yolen

A Spiritual Practice to Help You on Your Way

Be honest with yourself. Do this above all other spiritual practices. Honesty is at the heart of the practice of confession, common to many religious traditions. Confessing our false self helps us to find our true self. To help, consider looking at the spiritual tradition of confession in a new way, as offering and accepting your faults and misdeeds, in order to move past them.

Phyllis Tickle, contributing editor in religion to
Publishers Weekly and author of *The Divine Hours* series

"*One of my personal, spiritual priorities for the future is . . .*

To expend more disciplined time and thought on theology. I find that up to this point in my life I have managed to do two things that have led me to the present urgency. First, I have focused my study on how I as a single soul am to live before my God; and second, I have managed thereby to pretty well avoid articulating a personal credo that covers the hard, as well as the easy and received, issues. This new century, it seems to me, will demand that each communion and each observant within it determine how we live not as individual believers, but as individuals within believing bodies that are themselves member-parts of the body of believers."

—Phyllis Tickle

Did You Know?

The use of spiritual retreat—time spent away from normal, daily concerns, in order to focus on spiritual reflection—is common in many religious traditions. The Christian gospels speak of the forty days Jesus spent in the desert before his public ministry. Islam traces the origin of the revelation of the Qur'an to Muhammad's retreat on Mt. Hira. Siddhartha sat alone under the Bodhi Tree until he became a Buddha.

"*One image or allegory that encapsulates our common spiritual quest is . . .*

A gift from Native American tradition: The Cherokee taught, and I believe, that life and all the creatures, creations and experiences that compose it are like a spider web. Whatever touches any part of it causes a trembling in every other part."

—Phyllis Tickle

Every life is a spiritual conversation with the Divine.

(Space here for reflection.)

O how amiable are thy dwellings,
thou Lord of hosts!
My soul hath a desire and longing
to enter into the courts of the Lord;
my heart and my flesh rejoice in the
living God.

—Psalm 84:1–2

"One *spiritual insight that I would like to share with others as they think about their priorities on their path to a rewarding spiritual life is . . .*

The subtle shift in attitude that passing the millennium mark made in many of us. We who were looking forward and waiting with rather cosmic curiosity for the rolling over of the era have now become those whom the next waiters, a thousand years from now, will look back upon. When I look back at 1000 C.E., I am almost pitying of my forebears' ignorance, inhumanity and religiosity. Yet I now stand in relation to the future exactly where they have stood for me. I find that to be a ferocious and instructive thought, one that will not let me go."

—Phyllis Tickle

A Spiritual Practice to Help You on Your Way

Write your personal credo, or statement of fundamental beliefs—whether it's a sentence, or even just three or four single words—answering the questions: "What do I believe?" and "What do I live for?"

Lawrence Kushner, author of *Invisible Lines of Connection:
Sacred Stories of the Ordinary*[ii] and many other books

Single Handing

Sailing a big boat is one thing; sailing it alone is something else. There is no one who can help you, no one you can ask. You must be prepared to fix—or live with—every contingency. Worse than being at the mercy of the elements, you are at the mercy of yourself and whatever you cannot handle alone. No matter how carefully you think through the sail in advance, no matter how many backup systems you have arranged, inevitably, something will go wrong that requires immediate correction. You are then alone with your own ingenuity, fortitude, courage. What goes wrong could come from the sea, the wind, your own stupidity, the boat, the equipment, the sails. And it usually makes something else go wrong. And you are alone.

I was surprised, therefore, when a friend who's a licensed Coast Guard captain suggested, "Being a single hander is easy."

"Sure," I said, "maybe for you. But for those of us who are beginners, no way."

"Wrong," he teased, "it's really easy. All you have to do is walk forward to the bow, stoop down to where the mooring line is made fast to the cleat, untie that line and drop it in the water. Presto, you're a single hander!"

"What do you mean?" I asked.

"You can pick it up again immediately—you had a short sail. Or you can sail around the world before you come back to the mooring again.

"We're not talking about *whether or not* you have the nerve to single hand the boat. We're only talking about how long. Short sail, long sail, it doesn't matter. Either way, you're a single hander."

Moving along by the grace of a power we cannot see. Neither of the earth nor of the sky. Hovering between them. Belonging to neither. Going forth by yourself.

My friend's advice reminded me of an old legend about crossing the Red Sea. According to tradition, the waters did not split until one man, Nahshon ben Aminidab, walked into them up to his nostrils. God then said, "For *him*, I will split the sea."

The redemption, the miracle, the transformation, they are all in *your* hands. Or, more precisely, in letting go of whatever you are holding. You let go of the line and set forward into the sea. How else would you expect the voyage to begin?

Living Together on This Small Planet

"*Each of us as an individual longs to reach the Promised Land and to enjoy the fullness of the promise, yet it is only as a People, the human family, that we can hope to successfully negotiate the journey.*"

—Fr. M. Basil Pennington, ocso (see page 51)

Is Our Planet Getting Smaller?

IN MANY RESPECTS, THIS PLANET WE SHARE is smaller every day. Population growth has exploded in "the two-thirds world" (two-thirds of the world lives in "the third world"), making basic human resources (like food, clothing and shelter) scarce in many places. According to the Population Reference Bureau, world population increased by 4.4 billion people in the 20th century. The Associated Press recently reported that the average growth rate in the poorest countries is eight times higher than in wealthy countries. Even if you have not noticed it yet, the planet is getting smaller.

The internet is also making the world a much smaller place. We may "connect" with people in seconds now, from one end of the world to the other, inexpensively and quickly. The great growth in inexpensive air travel also makes it possible for us to communicate face-to-face with people thousands of miles away. And more than half a century without a world war has created a global environment of increasing peace and understanding between cultures—but of course, we still have a long way to go.

Our planet has gotten much smaller *religiously* in the past century, as well. Eastern religions arrived in North America little more than 150 years ago. But it was not really until the 1960s, through the books and lecturing of people like Ram Dass and Thich Nhat Hanh, that the West began to understand that Eastern spiritual traditions and practices are available all around us, not just in monasteries and the Far East. This influx of Eastern religion brought new life to spirituality in America. Since then, in the intervening 35–40 years, there is increasingly better understanding between faiths—concerning our differences as well as our similarities—but more importantly, all faiths have been enriched as those of us within them learn from each other.

What was completely unheard of only a few years ago is common-place today: We learn from spiritual leaders and religious traditions other than the one we call our own. We are interested in learning from a variety of sources, and the leaders and institutions of our religious traditions are less circumspect and more open to a variety of possible sources for spiritual understanding.

In most communities today in America, for the first time, neighbors, co-workers, families and friends represent different religious traditions. Baptists marry Buddhists, Jews marry Hindus, and we live and practice side-by-side. Spiritually and religiously, we communicate more closely with each other than ever before, and this is a good way in which the world is smaller than it used to be.

We Talk More and Listen Less

While the planet and the universe are smaller in these many ways, ironically, our world has lost much of its intimacy. In North America, suburban sprawl has eroded many traditional features of our communities, such as locally owned businesses and daily meeting places where we stay in touch with those we live the closest to. The creation of world media networks like CNN has been a great blessing for our understanding of the broader world, but this means of communication has also been a great detriment to our understanding of our *local* world. We tend to cocoon today, staying inside with the images and information on our TVs, the internet and e-mail; we find friends in cyberspace rather than meeting friends in public places in our communities.

Our Combined Potential

Only when we learn to see the Divine in others can we learn together, and grow together, on this small planet. Our differences define us, but it is our potential to be God's agents in the world that unites us.

Whether you strive to be a bodhisattva, a brahman, a better Christian or Jew, or simply a positive and conscious presence in the world, we all may work together to alleviate suffering, free slaves and "be places where God's love turns up in this world" (Fr. M. Basil Pennington, OCSO, see page 51).

Most people fall into one of four categories according to how they try to improve the planet. (Excluding, of course, those who don't even try.) Each type of person is critical to our group survival as we fight oppression, environmental insensitivity, violence, exploitative relationships, disease, homelessness, poverty and all of the dangers we face together. These four types of people are:

- **The Activist**—You roll up your sleeves and get directly involved in neighborhood education, national consciousness awareness efforts and projects where you invest time, sweat and a lot of energy to change damaging behavior and improve the planet.

- **The Householder**—You work diligently to sustain, restore and improve the world around you, believing that the way you live your life can either help or hurt the planet, and you choose to help.

- **The Evangelist**—You spread the truth about problems we all face, and motivate others to change what is wrong in the world.

- **The Utopian**—You create an environment where people who share your desires to improve the planet can join together and live in those concrete, specific and meaningful ways together.

After you have read the summaries of these four types of people, think about which type you most resemble in your beliefs—and in your actual behavior. How are you trying to improve the planet right now?

Sandy Eisenberg Sasso, the second woman to be ordained a rabbi (1974), author of *Cain & Abel: Finding the Fruits of Peace; God's Paintbrush; In God's Name* and other award-winning books for children

"One of my personal, spiritual priorities for the future is . . .

To recognize the interconnectedness of life in all its diversity, to see difference not in terms of superiority and inferiority. Each human face, each naming of the sacred, is a reflection of the One who includes us all. The more names, the more faces, we come to treasure, the closer we come to understand the One. I also want to stop and remember that no time is insignificant and that it is our responsibility to sanctify all times and places. I believe that we find ourselves in specific places at particular moments in order to redeem the holy sparks that reside there."

—Sandy Eisenberg Sasso

Did You Know?

Greeting the morning sun with prayer, chanting or meditation is a spiritual practice of many faith traditions ranging from the Tarahumara and Navajo Indians of North America to the ancient Jewish, Hindu and Christian traditions of morning prayer. Devout Muslims actually begin their cycle of daily prayer *before* sunrise.

"One image or allegory that encapsulates our common spiritual quest is . . .

The well. Our spiritual journeys have led us up mountains with Abraham to Moriah, Moses to Sinai, Elijah to Carmel. There were steep climbs and dizzy descents. But mountains and ladders with angels coming up and down do not find a resting place for the 21st-century soul. I prefer the image of the well. We ascend the mountain alone and feel powerful. Our vision is of superiority. We gather together and draw water from deep within the well and feel grateful. Our vision is of the shared good. If the traditional pilgrimage may be characterized as an ascent, then the pilgrimage to the well is an embrace."

—Sandy Eisenberg Sasso

Every life is a spiritual conversation with the Divine.
(Space here for reflection.)

Blessed are You, Adonai our God, ruler of the world, who forms light and creates darkness, makes peace and creates everything, illumining the earth and those who dwell there in mercy, in his goodness forever renewing daily the work of creation.

—From the "Blessing on Creation," a part of the traditional Jewish prayer service

"O*ne spiritual insight that I would like to share with others as they think about their priorities on their path to a rewarding spiritual life is . . .*

In our spiritual searching, I encourage us to take the hand of a child. If what is at the heart of spirituality is wonder, the ability to see the extraordinary in the ordinary, then who better to take our hand on our spiritual journey than our children? A wonderful story is told of a four-year-old who waits impatiently for the birth of a second child in the family. When the parents finally bring the infant home, they overhear their older child saying to the infant, 'Can you tell me about God? I am beginning to forget.' Children are not empty vessels into which we pour a religious spirit. They have a spiritual life and it is our privilege as adults not only to help nurture that life but to learn from it."

–Sandy Eisenberg Sasso

A Spiritual Practice to Help You on Your Way

If you are having trouble concentrating in prayer, or finding a quiet space for meditation—go for a walk. And invite the Divine to come along! Converse as you walk. Sometimes remembering to be "casual" in your relationship with the Divine (however you define it) may help you to "see the extraordinary in the ordinary."

Kathy Shaidle, author of *God Rides a Yamaha: Musings on Prayer, Poetry and Pop Culture*

"*One of my personal, spiritual priorities for the future is . . .*

Openness: open mind, open hands, open heart, open door. Millennium mania inspired lots of people to begin their spiritual searches. Calling myself a 'life-long seeker' sounds romantic and brave, but I will remain neurotic, lonely and self-absorbed unless I choose one path, one discipline, and stick with it through good times and bad. And I won't be allowed to keep the little wisdom I've acquired unless I share with others what I've been so freely given. I pray for the courage to stop searching and start standing, to keep what I have by giving it away."

—Kathy Shaidle

Did You Know?

There are rich religious traditions of respecting the earth. Most people know that St. Francis preached to the birds, honoring them as creatures of God and equals on the planet. But, did you know there is each year a Jewish holiday of *Tu b'Shevat*, the New Year of Trees? On this increasingly popular holiday, Jews celebrate nature in ways that begin to "fix" the universe and restore the collective soul that was broken when Adam and Eve ate the apple. In the West, *Tu b'Shevat* is celebrated each year in mid-winter.

"One image or allegory that encapsulates our common spiritual quest is . . .*

The labyrinth. Labyrinth walking was a Christian meditation technique that thrived centuries ago. Participants slowly and deliberately walk to the circle's center along a twisting path drawn on the ground, and then walk back out. (Usually taking 30 or so minutes to complete.) Labyrinths quietly slipped into disuse—the one at Chartres Cathedral closed 250 years ago—but today, thanks to the rediscovery of Christian meditation, there are more than 2,500 around the world. Perhaps the growing popularity of labyrinths indicates that they draw people of many levels and from many traditions. They also strike me as an elegant marriage of mind, body and soul, stillness and motion."

—Kathy Shaidle

Every life is a spiritual conversation with the Divine.

(Space here for reflection.)

> The dramatic threat of ecological breakdown is teaching us the extent to which greed and selfishness...are contrary to the order of Creation.
>
> —Pope John Paul II[iii]

"One spiritual insight that I would like to share with others as they think about their priorities on their path to a rewarding spiritual life is . . .

A story: The oldest monk in the desert knew his time to die was coming. One by one, he sold his meager possessions and gave the pennies to the poor. First his wobbly wooden stool, then his scratched bowl and bent spoon, then his tattered blanket. The younger monks looked on and nodded approvingly. But then the old monk sold his last and most treasured possession—his Bible. The younger monks ran to the old man's hut, shocked—and a little afraid. If the old man's sanity had left along with his furniture, then one of them would be stuck with the task of wiping his wrinkled old chin. They burst into the old monk's tent. He looked as sane as ever, maybe saner; still, the youngsters felt compelled to scold and question him. 'A rug or a pillow, that we can understand. But, how could you part with the very word of God?' The old man shrugged, then lay down for one last, everlasting sleep. He rolled over, turning from the others, and sighed just loud enough for only some of them to hear: 'All I did was sell the very book that told me to go and sell everything I have.'"

—Kathy Shaidle

A Spiritual Practice to Help You on Your Way

On a piece of paper—or in the margin here—write the name of someone you love dearly and whom you have known for more than five years. Below his/her name, write the two things you most want for him/her, and what or how you can give of yourself to help.

Father M. Basil Pennington, ocso,
author of *Lectio Divina* and *A Place Apart:*
Monastic Prayer and Practice for Everyone

“One *of my personal, spiritual priorities*
for the future is . . .

As it has always been, to grow in love—love of God, love of myself, my true self, and of my neighbor, who on this small intimately connected planet is every woman, man and child alive: to be a place where God's love turns up in this world.”

—Fr. M. Basil Pennington, ocso

Did You Know?

Religious holidays often follow lunar calendars, according to ancient traditions. The Christian holiday of Easter, for instance, is celebrated on the first Sunday after the first full moon of spring. Jewish holidays, including the weekly Sabbath, begin at sunset, because a lunar-based calendar is used. The Muslim holiday of Ramadan is celebrated for a full lunar month and may last 29 or 30 days depending on the cycle of the moon. The Gregorian calendar—in daily use by most of us throughout the world today—is a solar calendar, and was first introduced in 1582 by Pope Gregory XIII.

"One *image or allegory that encapsulates our* *common spiritual quest is . . .*

We are all the Pilgrim People. We have passed through the sea and received the Divine directives; we must continue on the journey. Each of us as an individual longs to reach the Promised Land and to enjoy the fullness of the promise, yet it is only as a People, the human family, that we can hope to successfully negotiate the journey with all its demands and do it joyfully in our shared love and celebration of who we are as the Pilgrim People."

—Fr. M. Basil Pennington, ocso

Every life is a spiritual conversation with the Divine.

(Space here for reflection.)

Someday, after mastering the winds, the waves, the tides and gravity, we shall harness for God the energies of love, and then for the second time in the history of the world, man *[sic]* will discover fire.

—Pierre Teilhard de Chardin[iv]

*"**O**ne spiritual insight that I would like to share with others as they think about their priorities on their path to a rewarding spiritual life is . . .*

No woman or man is an island. What each one of us does or does not do affects the rest of us. Each of us can be a bit of leaven which leavens the whole or we can be a bit of poison that makes the whole noxious. We can be a good cell that makes its contribution, maybe completely unseen, to the well-being of the whole, or be a cancer that seeks only its own growth to the ultimate detriment of all who surround it."

—Fr. M. Basil Pennington, ocso

A Spiritual Practice to Help You on Your Way

As a way to learn about mindfulness, spend today paying close attention to the noise you, personally, make in the world. Hear how you open and close doors. Hear how you talk with others. Hear the sounds that occur when you wash your hands. Now, practice washing your hands *mindfully*. Focus on the stillness in your soul where you meet the Divine.

Rodger Kamenetz, author of *Terra Infirma*
and *Stalking Elijah*

"*One of my personal, spiritual priorities for the future is . . .*

One—at least one!—of my priorities will certainly be to pay attention to what is happening in each holy moment, and to value especially the time I have left with loved ones and friends, and to know how precious and sweet life here is and can be."

—Rodger Kamenetz

Did You Know?

The tree is a common symbol in many religious traditions. In the mystical tradition of Islam, the tree has its roots in heaven, reaching down to us in order that we might become fruit.

*"*ne image or allegory that encapsulates our common spiritual quest is . . .*

Maimonides—the great Jewish medieval philosopher—speaks of those lucky souls for whom spiritual growth is a natural aptitude, and those more unfortunate (but no doubt more normative) souls whose task is to 'overcome their tendencies.' I am very sure I am in the latter category and the future will find me struggling with the same old obscurations: needless anger, despair, quick-trigger lusts, guilts, sorrows, greeds and an assortment of pesky minor irritabilities and peccadilloes."

—Rodger Kamenetz

Every life is a spiritual conversation with the Divine.
(Space here for reflection.)

Make clean, make glad, make
bright and make alive
my spirit, with all the powers
thereof, that I may
cleave unto thee in ecstasies of joy.

—A prayer of Thomas à Kempis
(1380–1471)

*"**O**ne spiritual insight that I would like to share with others as they think about their priorities on their path to a rewarding spiritual life is . . .*

One major problem is setting priorities and sticking to them and I don't know whether the thunderclap of a new calendar setting, with all those attractive zeroes rolling up on the group odometer as we travel together into unknown highways of time, will succeed in focusing me any better than the previous numerals of the 20th century did. But I hope we can all of us bring out more of the sweetness of the time we are sharing on this planet."

—Rodger Kamenetz

A Spiritual Practice to Help You on Your Way

Buddhist meditation speaks of the "Four Immeasurable Qualities" that open wide our hearts to really seeing the suffering around us. These are joy, love, equanimity and compassion. Concentrate on the emotions and behavior in your life that are keeping you separated from your own stores of joy, love, equanimity and compassion. These same masks of emotion and behavior also keep us from seeing the joy and suffering in the other people around us. What steps can you take today to get rid of one of those masks, to let yourself open your heart wider and increase your compassion?

Rabbi Arthur Waskow, director of the Shalom
Center; author of *Godwrestling—Round 2;*
Down-to-Earth Judaism and *Torah of the Earth:*
Exploring 4,000 Years of Ecology in Jewish Thought

"O*ne of my personal, spiritual priorities*
for the future is . . .

To gather together those who are pursuing the renewal (not restoration
of old versions) of Judaism, Christianity, Islam and Buddhism to share
their insights, concerns and prayers about our planet."

—Rabbi Arthur Waskow

Did You Know?

The little book *Tao Te Ching,* by Lao Tzu, was most likely
composed in the 6th century B.C.E. In 81 short, epigram-
matic chapters, Lao Tzu shows both a path to personal
enlightenment *and* how the enlightened can create a better
society. There is not one without the other.

"One image or allegory that encapsulates our common spiritual quest is . . .

Shabbat: Our need to rest and reflect not only as individuals but as a society—to reflect on the astounding, transformative and dangerous achievement in human Doing, Working, Making and Producing of the last half-millennium and take the time to Be, to Love and to Reflect in order to create new communal forms that can nurture our transforming planet."

—Rabbi Arthur Waskow

Every life is a spiritual conversation with the Divine.

(Space here for reflection.)

"Where is the center of the world?"
"Between your own two feet."

—An old Irish saying

“One spiritual insight that I would like to share with others as they think about their priorities on their path to a rewarding spiritual life is . . . PAUSE. REST. REFLECT.”

—Rabbi Arthur Waskow

A Spiritual Practice to Help You on Your Way

"The most direct means for attaching ourselves to God from this material world is through music and song. Even if you can't sing well, sing. Sing to yourself. Sing in the privacy of your own home. But sing."

—Rebbe Nachman of Breslov (1772–1810);
from *The Empty Chair*[v]

Rev. Theodore M. Hesburgh, CSC,
president emeritus, University of Notre Dame

"One of my personal, spiritual priorities for the future is . . .

To renew my commitment to the priesthood, to re-dedicate myself to all of the people of the world whom I encounter and to be open to the Spirit."

—Rev. Theodore M. Hesburgh, CSC

Did You Know?

"Redemption," "liberation" and "enlightenment" are not always about ourselves. In Christian tradition, redemption often refers to the process we are all in the midst of together—restoring the *world* to intimacy with God. In Mahayana Buddhism, the selfless daily laboring of women and men (called bodhisattvas) to lead others to enlightenment, shows a similar approach to "redeeming" the world.

"One image or allegory that encapsulates our common spiritual quest is . . .

To live our lives under the inspiration of the Holy Spirit. I want to be open to everyone seeking spiritual growth and even to those who don't realize what this is."

—Rev. Theodore M. Hesburgh, CSC

Every life is a spiritual conversation with the Divine.
(Space here for reflection.)

O God, make a light in my heart and a light in my tongue. Make a light in my ear; and make a light in my eye; make a light in back of me and a light in front of me; make a light above me. O God give me light.

—Abu Hamid al-Ghazali, a Muslim mystic (11th century)[vi]

" ***O****ne spiritual insight that I would like to share with others as they think about their priorities on their path to a rewarding spiritual life is . . .*

How we can grow spiritually: We all need the inspiration of the Holy Spirit, and a vision of what the world might be if all of us were faithful to the inspirations of the Spirit."

—Rev. Theodore M. Hesburgh, csc

A Spiritual Practice to Help You on Your Way

Mother Teresa frequently taught "the beginning of prayer is silence." It takes practice to be silent, to allow the Divine to speak in the quiet of our heart. Today, try to be silent for a while—silent with yourself and with God. For many of us this is one of the most difficult spiritual practices, but one that is worth the extra effort.

Living Together on This Small Planet:
A Story from...

Tamar Frankiel and Judy Greenfeld, authors of
*Minding the Temple of the Soul: Balancing Body, Mind,
and Spirit through Traditional Jewish Prayer, Movement,
and Meditation*[vii]

Story of a Soul

"Soul," said God, "I have a mission for you."

A mission? The Soul thought only angels had missions. "Yes, I'm ready," the Soul said aloud.

"You will go to earth for a certain period of time," God proclaimed.

"Earth? From what the angels say, it's dark and heavy there."

"Yes, compared to where you are. One of your jobs will be to bring light there."

"How do I do that?"

"You will receive instruction," said God. "There will be time set aside for that."

"What is time?" the Soul asked.

God sighed. "It's very hard to explain, but when you're in it, you'll know it."

"Whatever you say," replied the Soul.

"You will also receive what you need to help you complete your mission," God continued. "It will also be hard to understand at first, but you'll have plenty of time to get used to it."

"You're talking about time again."

"All right. The point is, I am giving you something unique for your mission on earth. It is called a body."

"Thank you. But what is a body? No, I guess there's no point asking. I'll find out."

"That's right. Remember, the main thing is not to fear."

In a flash, the Soul found itself in a strange situation. It seemed to be in a kind of cave, smooth and soft all around. The energy was dense, but the Soul moved through it easily. At the same time, there was an embracing warmth, almost like being in the presence of the Creator.

Then an angel appeared, a presence of gentle light. The angel lit a candle and opened an immense book. The angel explained that the Soul was now inhabiting a body, and would soon enter into the human world as a tiny member of the human species. The Soul listened and began to understand the wondrous purposes of existence, and the special role it would have in its earthly life. The angel also gave instructions, explaining how the Soul could stay connected with the spiritual world it had temporarily left behind. The knowledge was delicious—the Soul could even taste it. The Soul felt radiant with joy.

The angel gazed sweetly at the Soul, kissed it on its upper lip, just below the nose and, before the Soul could speak, disappeared. Warm darkness surrounded the Soul, and it slipped into a deep, restful sleep.

When it awoke, the Soul realized that its body was going through a great change. There was pressure and movement. The Soul wondered what was happening, and tried to remember what the angel had said. There was something about beginning a mission—but what were the instructions the angel had given? The Soul suddenly realized its clarity of understanding was gone.

Panic rose, and the Soul wanted to escape.

"Remember, the main thing is not to fear," an inner voice said.

The Soul quieted itself. But the urge to get out was strong. As the thoughts of escape grew louder, the Soul suddenly found itself being pushed with a mighty force into what seemed to be a tunnel. In a moment it was sliding down a canal toward a glimmer of light that reminded the Soul ever so slightly of home.

What a lift that small bit of light gave the Soul! Then a breeze swept through, a delicious breath of life, followed by a vibration, a sound that came from its own body. A moment later, the body was completely embraced, held, and rocked with a gentle motion. The Soul could focus now, and saw faces and eyes, almost as sweet as the angel's. Voices, one low and one high, spoke nearby, and the happy words were like music. Those loving voices also reminded the Soul of the warmth and love of the Soul World. The Soul felt a great delight.

The surrounding energy began to settle into a calmer, more regular movement. Warmth now flowed into the body, a sweet-tasting liquid. Lips and fingers moved on soft, warm skin. The fragrances of body, milk, and fabric were a kaleidoscope, changing each moment.

The Soul was thrilled at this new beginning for its life. It poured its light into all these sensations, longing to express its surprise and happiness. Its eyes opened and sent a loving look to the eyes that gazed back with a smile.

The Soul knew that a great miracle had occurred, and sent a thankful song back to...whoever had brought it to this experience.

The Soul realized that the past, and all the places it had been, had become very hazy now. The Soul hoped it would find a way to remember.

Co-Creating
with the Divine

" *Spiritual practice is not about transformation of me, or of anyone else, as individuals—the job is too big and that purpose is too small. We practice to transform the world.* "

—Sylvia Boorstein (see page 73)

What Does It Mean to Be Co-Creators?

EACH ONE OF US IS IN THE PROCESS of spiritual growth from the moment we are born until death and beyond. And part of spiritual growth is understanding that our spiritual paths are not just about ourselves. As Sylvia Boorstein reminds us in this section, "we practice to transform the world." Spiritual teachings and spiritual growth, if they really take root, always lead to new fruit, which shows itself in new or renewed practice. Central to our "spiritual practice" (the ways we express our spirituality) must be the question of how and where it enables us to co-create the world that surrounds us.

Spiritual practice that is primarily personal (like meditation, for instance) is not necessarily exclusively so. All practice has the power to not only change your life, but the lives of others. The *subject* of most spiritual practice is you—but don't assume that you know the *object!*

One example of personal, spiritual practice that transformed the world was the way that Mahatma Gandhi (1869–1948), the Indian nationalist and spiritual leader, used fasting, silence and solitude to create a new consciousness in both his friends and foes. Gandhi's story is well known. He spent many months, and cumulative years, in jail in both South Africa and his native India. He often fasted in prison, which infuriated his incarcerators, who viewed it as a weapon used to win public support. It *was* that, in its effect, but this was also Gandhi's powerful spiritual practice, which heightened the awareness—both spiritual and political—of his people.

Is it any coincidence that Gandhi both loved silence and solitude and carried out political action that he knew would result in his imprisonment? He used the time alone to strengthen his practice. His political life was inseparable from his spiritual life. His time alone not only strengthened him, but others. His love for silence, enhanced in prison, even led Gandhi to maintain one full day a week in complete silence when he was not in prison.

What can we learn from Gandhi's spiritual practice? He practiced so consciously that its effect reached a nation, and the world. Personal practice often does this—in smaller ways. Our individual practices change the world. When I meditate in stillness the world becomes more still. When I fast in devotion the world is less hungry. When I…

Of course, there is also spiritual practice that is overtly aimed at transforming the world. For example, the "engaged Buddhism" of people like Bernie Glassman (Zen Peacemaker Order) and Joan Halifax (Project on Being with Dying) are mirrored by efforts in other religious traditions to actively engage in both practice and care for others. According to the Jewish mystic tradition, our responsibility is to release the holy sparks—the Divine potentialities in every thing in the universe—by *engagement* with the world. That is what this section, "Co-Creating with the Divine," is all about.

Co-creating with the Divine involves first seeing ourselves as actors in our spiritual lives, and in creating the future of the planet.

This simple self-test is intended to help you focus on what the current state of your spiritual practice is.

Answer each question with a numerical value:

1. I see myself as a partner with God in the world.	**1 2 3 4 5**
2. I see myself as a creation of God.	**1 2 3 4 5**
3. I see God as mostly separate from my daily life.	**1 2 3 4 5**
4. I understand my spiritual life most when I discuss spiritual matters with others.	**1 2 3 4 5**
5. I understand my spiritual life most by studying and talking with God.	**1 2 3 4 5**
6. My personal "spiritual practice"—the ways in which I express my spirituality—is what makes my spiritual life meaningful.	**1 2 3 4 5**

1 = Never; 2 = Occasionally; 3 = Fairly often; 4 = Very often; 5 = Always

Add your scores to questions 1 and 4 together (Grouping A), to 2 and 5 together (Grouping B), and to 3 and 6 together (Grouping C).

Whichever grouping scores the highest points represents your current view of spiritual relationships.

Grouping A Your spiritual practice is highly interactive. You are consciously working with others to transform the world around you.

Grouping B You gain most of your spiritual strength through your direct relationship with God. Practice is probably secondary in importance for you.

Grouping C Your spirituality is focused primarily on personal practice. The effect of your practice on others is subtle, rather than obvious.

Sylvia Boorstein, author of *It's Easier Than You Think: The Buddhist Way to Happiness* and co-founding teacher at Spirit Rock Meditation Center

"One of my personal, spiritual priorities for the future is . . .

To remind myself and teach everyone I meet about clarity of intention. Spiritual practice is not about transformation of me, or of anyone else, as individuals—the job is too big and that purpose is too small. I trust that establishing kindness and compassion in any of our individual hearts is on behalf of all beings everywhere. We practice to transform the world."

—Sylvia Boorstein

Did You Know?

Confucius spoke of the virtue of "jen," or human-heartedness, the love and altruism we all should strive for. Literally, in Chinese, "jen" means the most essentially human part of us expressing itself as virtue for others. It is the essentially human, in Confucianism, that is spiritual.

"**O**ne image or allegory that encapsulates our common spiritual quest is . . .

Shared homework. This *world* has homework. How will we keep our air and water clean? How will we distribute the world's resources more equitably so that our children and grandchildren inherit a non-violent, habitable world? How will we recognize, appreciate and respect cultural and religious differences *as well as* our shared human desire for lives of peace and happiness?"

—Sylvia Boorstein

Every life is a spiritual conversation with the Divine.

(Space here for reflection.)

You are the salt of the earth; but if salt has lost its taste, how can its saltiness be restored?

—Jesus of Nazareth, from "The Sermon on the Mount"

*"*__O__*ne spiritual insight that I would like to share with others as they think about their priorities on their path to a rewarding spiritual life is . . .*

We do not wake up to wisdom once-and-for-all-and-forever. This insight has become increasingly clear to me. Nevertheless, I trust that a lifetime of practice dedicated to retraining mind-habits of greed, hatred and delusion to kindness, compassion and clarity makes a difference."

—Sylvia Boorstein

A Spiritual Practice to Help You on Your Way

Spend each day of the next week asking people to tell you their stories. Choose one friend, co-worker or acquaintance each day and ask: *Tell me something about yourself: a time you were enlightened, uncomfortable, most happy.* Listen carefully to the story you get. Share your stories in return. By really listening to the stories of our lives, we find God.

Dr. Bernie Siegel, author of *Love, Medicine and Miracles* and *Prescriptions for Living*

"*One of my personal, spiritual priorities for the future is . . .*
To be a loving human being."

—Dr. Bernie Siegel

A period of forty days is used in various spiritual traditions to signify a time of discipline, devotion, contemplation and even suffering. In the Hebrew scriptures, we are told that Moses spent two forty-day periods on Mt. Sinai, receiving God's revelations. Noah and his family suffered through forty days and forty nights of punishing downpour. Elijah fasted for forty days on his journey to Mt. Horeb. Even the giant Goliath taunted Israel for forty days. In the Christian tradition, the forty days that Jesus spent fasting in the wilderness are commemorated in the penitential season of Lent, a period of fasting and prayer that is spiritual preparation for the passion, death and resurrection of Christ celebrated on Easter Sunday. The traditions of Sufism, too, encourage meditation and prayer retreats lasting forty days.

"One image or allegory that encapsulates our common spiritual quest is . . .

We are all the same color inside, have the same parents (Adam and Eve), and Creator."

—Dr. Bernie Siegel

Every life is a spiritual conversation with the Divine.

(Space here for reflection.)

Praise to God and compassion
for creatures.
It is the same movement of
the heart.

—Simone Weil, from *First and
Last Notebooks*

"One spiritual insight that I would like to share with others as they think about their priorities on their path to a rewarding spiritual life is . . .

Decide which Lord you work for. We are here to be co-creators."

—Dr. Bernie Siegel

A Spiritual Practice to Help You on Your Way

Consider what you consume in an average week. Now consider that food, fuel, clothing, water and other essentials are in short supply worldwide. For instance, the average North American family spends about 15% of take-home pay on food, but in Haiti, that number is 75–80%.

Are there ways that you can reduce your consumption of essential resources (perhaps without even noticeably affecting your lifestyle)? Try it. Total the financial savings of living with less and spend that money to help the less fortunate.

Dr. Eugene Fisher, for the National Council of Synagogues and the National Conference of Catholic Bishops

"Three of our personal, spiritual priorities for the future are . . .

- Confront the inhuman conditions of bigotry, exploitation and violence that enslave such a large part of America's inhabitants.

- Introduce moral guidance into economics.

- Nurture and care for all forms of life.

These obligations have significance, we believe not only for Catholics and Jews working together in joint study and action, but also for the renewal of our American society as a whole."

—Dr. Eugene Fisher

Did You Know?

Oscar Romero (1917–1980), Roman Catholic Archbishop of El Salvador, grew to be hated by those in El Salvador embarrassed by his insistence on speaking out on behalf of those murdered by both government and guerrilla forces during the bloody civil unrest there. He was assassinated in 1980 as he said mass in a hospital chapel.

"One image or allegory that encapsulates our common spiritual quest is . . .

We work together to prepare the way for the coming of the Reign ('king-dom') of God."

—Dr. Eugene Fisher

Every life is a spiritual conversation with the Divine.
(Space here for reflection.)

> Where the mind is led forward by Thee into ever-widening thought and action—
> Into that heaven of freedom, my Father, let my country awake.
>
> —Rabindranath Tagore
> (1861–1941)

*"*One spiritual insight that we would like to share with others as they think about their priorities on their path to a rewarding spiritual life is . . .*

We speak at the end of a century that Pope John Paul II has called 'the Century of the Shoah.' Because of our dialogue, and commitment to continuing it, we can look forward to the next century with greater hope and confidence than might have been thought possible just a generation ago."

—Dr. Eugene Fisher

A Spiritual Practice to Help You on Your Way

We often think of prayer as a practice simply aimed at petitioning God for things we want; for instance, if we are sick, we ask God for help. We rarely experience the effects of prayer on this level, and so we get tired of praying altogether. Try looking at prayer differently: View it as a practice that aims to change your life not by Divine intervention, but by creating a more humble, devoted spirit in *you*. The purpose of prayer is to change *you*, not your circumstances.

Rt. Rev. Krister Stendahl, bishop emeritus
of Stockholm and former dean of Harvard
Divinity School

"One of my personal, spiritual priorities
for the future is . . .

As I shall not live long into the second millennium—as Christians count
'the years of our Lord,' *anno domini*—my desire is to understand ever
more fully this verse from Paul's letter to the church in Corinth: '...but
we all with unveiled faces beholding the glory of the Lord are being
changed from glory to glory into that image [in which we were creat-
ed]—and that by the Lord, the Spirit.'"

—Rt. Rev. Krister Stendahl

Did You Know?

Celtic monks in the Middle Ages often viewed
their spirituality as a life of wandering, and sometimes literally set out to sea in an oarless boat,
called a *curach*, allowing the wind and waves to set
their course.

"One image or allegory that encapsulates our common spiritual quest is . . .

Holy Envy. If we can love our neighbor only by what we have in common, then there is little hope for peace in the world—and in our souls. Hence our spirituality must be capable of Holy Envy: to have an eye for, and to admit without hesitation or defensiveness, what is beautiful in the Other—but it is not ours; nor should we try to make it our own. It would be just cut flowers without roots in our garden. Without such Holy Envy there can be no lasting spiritual health. Is not our common humanity a sufficiently compelling bond for neighborliness?"

—Rt. Rev. Krister Stendahl

Every life is a spiritual conversation with the Divine.
(Space here for reflection.)

Human beings are God's language.

—Hasidic saying

"One spiritual insight that I would like to share with others as they think about their priorities on their path to a rewarding spiritual life is . . .

I have come to recognize the urgent wisdom of those who want to turn the old formula around and say: How much diversity do we need? How much unity can we afford? Otherwise we violate the Other in the name of claiming universality."

—Rt. Rev. Krister Stendahl

A Spiritual Practice to Help You on Your Way

When was the last time you visited a religious service from another faith tradition? Exploring how people of other faiths worship can enhance your practice, in your tradition. Ask a friend if you may join him or her at an upcoming service or ceremony. Go and listen respectfully (ask your friend when it is appropriate to participate).

Patrick Marrin, editor, Celebration Publications,
the National Catholic Reporter Publishing Co.

*" **O***ne of my personal, spiritual priorities
for the future is . . .*

To try and stay focused on new beginnings—what comes next and what
challenges and opportunities it holds—rather than looking back. The
best spiritual advice I ever received was to always go forward."

—Patrick Marrin

Did You Know?

Central to Jewish spirituality is the idea of *tikkun
olam,* the act of "repairing the world." Our responsibility is to do this daily, in every big and little
thing we do.

"One image or allegory that encapsulates our common spiritual quest is . . .

The idea that, just as evolution proceeds through natural selection, human beings must evolve through dialogue. Creative solutions to our common problems will emerge from full and open dialogue among the diverse voices representing the total human experience. No one group has all the answers. To exclude any voice is to limit our future, even to risk extinction."

—Patrick Marrin

Every life is a spiritual conversation with the Divine.
(Space here for reflection.)

> Each person is responsible for the rise and fall of the world.
>
> —Confucius

"One spiritual insight that I would like to share with others as they think about their priorities on their path to a rewarding spiritual life is . . .

There can be no peace, no compassion, without justice. This is as true for individuals as for large social systems. If we are not at peace, it usually means that there are unresolved justice issues in our personal lives, relationships, professional careers. Seek justice and joy will follow."

—Patrick Marrin

A Spiritual Practice to Help You on Your Way

The practice of offering and receiving spiritual direction is common across religious traditions. Sometimes a spiritual teacher, or simply a fellow seeker, will guide another person, offering spiritual advice and example. Spiritual directors take many forms—teachers, friends, books. We all need them. The point of spiritual direction is simple: You can know your God only if you first know yourself. Think about this: Who and what are the spiritual directors in your life right now? Should you seek out more—or focus more deeply on one?

What Is a Time Capsule?

We often share hopes and aspirations with others. We also have hopes not shared, because for whatever reason they are too personal. In both cases, we need to set goals and priorities for ourselves. The old saying goes that no matter if you believe you will succeed, or if you believe you will fail, you probably are right either way. The point is, we make happen the things we focus our attention on, much more often that those things we only dream about. A time capsule offers us a way to focus on our hopes in a concrete way.

A Five-Year Time Capsule: Your Spiritual Goals

Set some of your spiritual goals for the next five years and file them away, stash them in a safe deposit box, tuck them under your mattress—wherever they will safely lie until you open them again five years from now. Or, you may prefer to mail them to a close friend, asking her/him to mail them back to you in five years. Or, keep them in a notebook or in a desk where you will see them every few months and can regularly chart your progress.

You may wish to use a separate piece of paper to fill out your Five-Year Time Capsule. If so, you may photocopy this page for that purpose. Answer these questions for yourself:

Five-Year Time Capsule

My Spiritual Goals

The answers below represent spiritual goals I have for myself, to be accomplished/attained between today, _____ (today's date), and 5 years from today, _____. I am writing them here to reinforce their importance for my life, and in the lives of every person who comes in contact with me.

1. Four spiritual lives I most admire are:

a)_____   b)_____

c)_____   d)_____

2. One spiritual quality I admire about each of these people, and that I want to cultivate in my own spiritual life, is:

a)_____   b)_____

c)_____   d)_____

3. I want to help the following people grow spiritually over the next five years:

a)_____   b)_____

c)_____   d)_____

4. To accomplish #3, I will take the following steps:

a)_____   b)_____

c)_____   d)_____

Focusing on What Is Most Important in Life

> **"O**ne spiritual insight that I would like to share with others as they think about their priorities on their path to a rewarding spiritual life is that an ordinary life, a humble one, given entirely to prayer and good works can have an impact and a radiance beyond the boundaries of the imaginable, and spark in others the fire of love and compassion, of generosity and selflessness, of peace and justice. These things are contagious."

—Br. Victor-Antoine d'Avila-Latourrette (see page 102)

How Do You Decide What Is Most Important in Life?

ONE OF THE MOST IMPORTANT THINGS TO REMEMBER in our spiritual lives is that we have choices. Regardless of our income level or our past or any other aspect of our life, we have decisions to make about how we will live now.

To use our choice-making capacity to improve our spiritual lives, we must first remember to live consciously. Living consciously means, first of all, avoiding the tendency to allow yourself to float thoughtlessly through life. Others will make decisions for you, if you don't make them yourself.

The following exercise helps to teach us to live consciously and reflectively.

Create a lifeline of choices you have made since high school. (Don't include choices *made for you*.) On one large piece of paper draw a line like a river on a map, followed by a branch for each major life choice you have made, and an opposite branch (moving the other direction) for the direction not taken. Label each with a phrase of description.

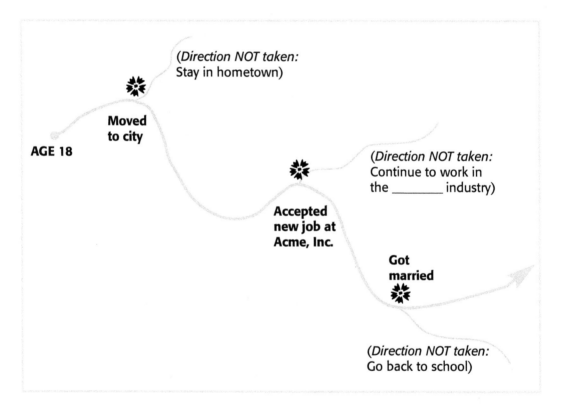

Reflect on your lifeline course. Focus especially on the fact that many "not-taken" branches exist on your life's course; focus also on the flexibility that is *inherent* in the course: You can take a new direction at any time—today, if you choose to.

Life Is Serious Business

A lifeline course shows us that there are key moments in our lives where one decision made all the difference. It also shows us that we each have a unique spiritual path.

In one of his talks to the monks at Gethsemani, Thomas Merton once said something similar when he told the monks that they each must find the unique way in which they will be Christ. Using his monastic name by which he was known in the monastery, he said that he was "Louie-Christ." The same idea is true in other religious traditions. How will you be Buddha? How will you realize Brahman? How will you hear God's voice?

The Important Things in Life

This book is full of examples of what is important for our spiritual lives. We may also look back at the 20th century for a sampling of ideas and movements that have recently helped to change the way we see the world. Consider how these concepts have affected our thinking or awareness or priorities in the past century: Twelve Steps, Earth Day, Liberation Theology, Amnesty International, Women Clergy, *Satyagraha,* Alternative Healing—your list may be different, but the list could go on and on.

It is our job now to decide what will be important in the next century, individually and globally.

Father Joseph F. Girzone, author of *A Portrait of Jesus,* the *Joshua* series and many other books

❝One *of my personal, spiritual priorities for the future is . . .*

To keep focused on what is essential. As a believer it is important to be sensitive to what is important to God and not what is expedient."

—Fr. Joseph F. Girzone

Did You Know?

Zen Buddhism shakes the foundations of most Western religious thought. In Zen, enlightenment comes only when we put away scriptures, only when we disregard our intelligence, only when we stop thinking and instead practice.

"One image or allegory that encapsulates our common spiritual quest is . . .

Christians, Jews and Muslims each claim the Temple Mount and Jerusalem as spiritual home, feeling only they have a right to be there. Only when the three accept each other and worship God together will God be pleased. That is true not only of Jerusalem but of our life together."

—Fr. Joseph F. Girzone

Every life is a spiritual conversation with the Divine.

(Space here for reflection.)

May the blessing of the great rains be on you,
to beat upon your spirit and wash it fair and clean;
and leave there many a shining pool
where the blue of heaven shines,
and sometimes a star.

—An Irish blessing[viii]

"One spiritual insight that I would like to share with others as they think about their priorities on their path to a rewarding spiritual life is . . .

God is not a God of nightmares and terror. God is a loving Creator who watches over us. To realize this and respond to that love dispels all fear of the future and inspires hope and longing for what God has prepared for us."

—Fr. Joseph F. Girzone

A Spiritual Practice to Help You on Your Way

Some people spend a lifetime dreaming of visiting a particular place, feeling that their life would be enriched or blessed from the experience of being there, praying there—or simply in the journey to it. This yearning is called the spirit of pilgrimage. Consider satisfying your yearning—and experiencing the small miracles that may await you there. Where will you go?

Dr. Andrew Weil, author of *Spontaneous Healing* and *8 Weeks to Optimum Health*

"One of my personal, spiritual priorities for the future is . . .

To continue to try to accept that everything in life is as it should be."

—Dr. Andrew Weil

Did You Know?

Tolstoy tells a beautiful tale of "The Three Hermits"—little, devout, aged men living on an island together, who one day are visited by a bishop. The bishop had heard of these men and thought it his duty to teach them a little bit of religion—the Lord's Prayer—even though the men had created a prayer of their own, which they prayed often together. After spending the day, feeling he'd served the hermits well, the bishop set sail again. Within an hour or two of leaving the island, the bishop saw three figures running across the water toward the ship. The three hermits reached the ship and reverently asked the bishop for more teaching—they had forgotten his prayer.

"One image or allegory that encapsulates our common spiritual quest is . . .

The transformation of the caterpillar into a butterfly."

—Dr. Andrew Weil

Every life is a spiritual conversation with the Divine.

(Space here for reflection.)

When the heart weeps for what it has lost, the spirit laughs for what it has found.

—A Sufi saying

*"*One spiritual insight that I would like to share with others as they think about their priorities on their path to a rewarding spiritual life is . . .*

The way to change the world is by changing yourself."

—Dr. Andrew Weil

A Spiritual Practice to Help You on Your Way

Perhaps the primary question answered differently by each major religion is: "How are we in bondage, and how can we get out?" On a separate piece of paper, or in the margin here, write down what you need to be set free from.

Brother Victor-Antoine d'Avila-Latourrette,
author of *Fresh from a Monastery Garden* and
Twelve Months of Monastery Soups

"One of my personal, spiritual priorities for the future is . . .

To strive for greater simplicity in lifestyle, in my prayer, in my pattern of thinking, in my relationships with other human beings, with the animals and the plants that I care for at the monastery. This simplicity hopefully will also be reflected in my writings, helping me to focus on the essential, thus trying to achieve greater unity of purpose."

—Br. Victor-Antoine d'Avila-Latourrette

Did You Know?

The lotus flower—a water plant native to Asia—is a powerful religious symbol in Hinduism and Buddhism. The lotus represents the goal of the spiritual life—to live beautifully in the world by avoiding attachment to the things of the world. (A lotus is rooted at the bottom of a pool, but flowers on the surface.)

"One image or allegory that encapsulates our common spiritual quest is . . .

The unity and harmony of the world we live in and that is entrusted to our stewardship by the Creator. Is it too much to hope for that a new millennium will have the force to awake in all of us a sense of a new era, an era where a renewed humanity will be capable of living in peace and harmony, rejecting violence, hatred, prejudice, greed, revenge, intolerance and discrimination of all sorts and kinds? The image that encapsulates best for me this ideal is that of the garden of Eden in the Bible, where man and woman walk in harmony with God, and with all the living creatures that God created."

—Br. Victor-Antoine d'Avila-Latourrette

Every life is a spiritual conversation with the Divine.

(Space here for reflection.)

> At the beginning of time I declared two paths for the pure heart, the intuitive path of spiritual wisdom and the active path of selfless service.
>
> —Sri Krishna, The Bhagavad Gita[ix]

"*One spiritual insight that I would like to share with others as they think about their priorities on their path to a rewarding spiritual life is . . .*

That an ordinary life, a humble one, given entirely to prayer and good works can have an impact and a radiance beyond the boundaries of the imaginable, and spark in others the fire of love and compassion, of generosity and selflessness, of peace and justice. These things are contagious."

—Br. Victor-Antoine d'Avila-Latourrette

A Spiritual Practice to Help You on Your Way

A spiritual retreat helps us to focus on what is important by stripping away all that is not. You can take a retreat with others at a retreat center or monastery, or you can take a retreat at home, alone. Most religions have strong traditions in both kinds of spiritual retreat. Take a retreat in your chosen tradition, but read also about other traditions' retreats, and consider what lessons *they* may hold for you as well. (A good resource for information on retreats is David A. Cooper's helpful book *Silence, Simplicity & Solitude: A Complete Guide to Spiritual Retreat at Home.*)

Katherine Paterson, author of *Jip: His Story*
and *Jacob Have I Loved*

"One of my personal, spiritual priorities for the future is . . .

To become more aware, more mindful, of persons, things and spirit."

—Katherine Paterson

Did You Know?

One of the most popular Zen tales tells of a man who is pursued by a tiger. He runs frantically trying to escape the beast. Upon reaching a cliff, he climbs down the side, holding for dear life onto a hanging vine. The tiger looks viciously over the side, and it seems that the vine will not hold for long. At that moment, the man sees fragrant, red strawberries growing within reach. He plucks one. "How sweet it tasted!" concludes the tale.[x]

"One image or allegory that encapsulates our common spiritual quest is . . .

The body where, as St. Paul reminds us, each has a different function but all are equally significant and any thing that happens to any part affects the whole."

—Katherine Paterson

Every life is a spiritual conversation with the Divine.

(Space here for reflection.)

O thou who camest from above,
The pure celestial fire to impart,
Kindle a flame of sacred love
On the mean altar of my heart.

There let it for thy glory burn
With inextinguishable blaze,
And trembling to its source return
In humble prayer, and fervent praise.

—A hymn of Charles Wesley (1707–1788)

“One spiritual insight that I would like to share with others as they think about their priorities on their path to a rewarding spiritual life is . . .

God loves and honors each one of us and wills that we should love and honor one another.”

—Katherine Paterson

A Spiritual Practice to Help You on Your Way

Places of worship (mosques, churches, synagogues) are usually sanctified to Divine work, meaning that in a formal way, with special prayers spoken, the building itself is "set apart" as a sacred space. Our homes, too, may be declared by us to be places where the Sacred is found and cultivated. The Jewish tradition offers a good example, where families nail to their exterior doorpost a *mezuzah*—a tiny case containing a parchment inscribed with verses from the book of Deuteronomy. Create your own ways of designating and shaping sacred space in your surroundings.

Mitch Finley, author of *Prayer for People Who Think Too Much* and *The Joy of Being Catholic*

"One of my personal, spiritual priorities for the future is . . .

To better integrate my spiritual/religious values and my everyday life."

—Mitch Finley

Did You Know?

Most faith traditions have what are called "liturgical calendars," or scheduled times throughout the year for believers to express their faith in ritual, through holidays and celebrations. Involvement in a faith tradition in this way can be very spiritually rewarding. In Christianity, for instance, it is no accident that Christmas is at the darkest time of year, and Easter, which celebrates new life, happens each year in spring.

"*One image or allegory that encapsulates our common spiritual quest is . . .*

Pilgrimage. During the Middle Ages it was popular for Christians to 'make a pilgrimage' to various sites all over Europe. The idea was to walk to a holy place to pray there, but the journey itself was a form of prayer. Even today people make pilgrimages to holy places (e.g., Mecca, Lourdes). A pilgrimage is a metaphor for the believer's 'sojourn' in this world, the ultimate goal of which is eternity. The pilgrimage reminds the pilgrim of the transitoriness of this life and of the need to live with the ultimate goal in mind—union with God."

—Mitch Finley

Every life is a spiritual conversation with the Divine.
(Space here for reflection.)

In the beginning was God,
Today is God,
Tomorrow will be God.
Who can make an image of God?
He has no body.
He is the word which comes out of your mouth.
That word! It is no more,
It is past, and still it lives!
So is God.

—A Pygmy hymn (African)[xi]

> **"O**ne spiritual insight that I would like to share
> with others as they think about their priorities
> on their path to a rewarding spiritual life is . . .
>
> Distrust the popular distrust of organized/institutional religion."
>
> —Mitch Finley

A Spiritual Practice to Help You on Your Way

In religion—as opposed to spirituality—people tend to write things down that a community can use to express itself together. That is usually how scriptures, commentaries and prayer books come to be—rich spiritual resources in every faith tradition. You may need to look again at the scriptures and prayers of religion to see them as if for the first time, with your eyes open to the riches they have to offer to your own spiritual way.

Frederic and Mary Ann Brussat, book and media reviewers for *Spirituality & Health* magazine and spiritualrx.com and authors of *Spiritual Literacy*

"*One of our personal, spiritual priorities for the future is . . .*

To continue reading and exploring the wide variety of resources—books, videos, spoken-word audios, Internet sites—reflecting the depth and breadth of today's spiritual renaissance. Regular study is recommended in most of the world's religions. For us, this means that we need to expose ourselves to many understandings and practices as we endeavor to live a spiritual life every day."

—Frederic and Mary Ann Brussat

Did You Know?

In most religious traditions, spiritual leaders recommend that you focus on one particular faith or path and grow in it. Many of us are good at spirituality shopping—but never settle into a tradition where our practice can grow and bear fruit. Sri Swami Satchidananda, founder of Integral Yoga Institutes Worldwide, recently said, "You may draw from the practices of various paths and faiths, but integrate them into one unified and harmonious path. Then follow that spiritual path with your goal in mind and stay with it consistently."[xii]

"One image or allegory that encapsulates our common spiritual quest is . . .

The path of practice. To us, this path is not restrictive in the way it is often described—as the straight and narrow or the steep and difficult climb up the mountain. We think of the path of practice as being a very broad boulevard. Sometimes it appears to be like a progressing line connecting two points. Other times it circles or spirals back on itself. There are no obvious intersections of roads taken and not taken because every avenue is connected and overlapping. Although there are places along the path of practice where you can be still and alone, usually it is packed with people and beings, animate and inanimate, visible and invisible, of our time and all times."

—Frederic and Mary Ann Brussat

Every life is a spiritual conversation with the Divine.
(Space here for reflection.)

Father in heaven! When the thought of thee wakes in our hearts let it not awaken like a frightened bird that flies about in dismay, but like a child waking from sleep with a heavenly smile.

—Søren Kierkegaard (1813–1855)

66 **O***ne spiritual insight that I would like to share with others as they think about their priorities on their path to a rewarding spiritual life is . . .*

The importance of practicing hospitality toward all religious and spiritual traditions. Separateness is an illusion, especially in the spiritual life."

—Frederic and Mary Ann Brussat

A Spiritual Practice to Help You on Your Way

"We suggest this exercise to build empathy and a feeling of unity with others. Whenever you find yourself making a judgment about someone—negative or positive—add the phrase 'just like me.' For example: 'She is so selfish, just like me.' 'He is so generous, just like me.'"

—Frederic and Mary Ann Brussat

Establishing Your Spiritual Priorities

Now It's Your Turn

YOU HAVE MOST LIKELY BEGUN renewing your spiritual priorities and purpose throughout the course of reading this book. In the previous pages, 23 spiritual teachers and writers have answered the same three questions—now it's your turn:

"One of my personal, spiritual priorities for the future is...

"One image or allegory that encapsulates our common spiritual quest is...

_____

_____

_____

_____

_____

_____

"One spiritual insight that I would like to share with others as they think about their priorities on their path to a rewarding spiritual life is . . .

_____

_____

_____

_____

_____

_____

Share with Us

We would like to read your answers to these questions—and hear what you have learned from *Forty Days to Begin a Spiritual Life*. We would also like to post your answers and comments on our website (www.skylightpaths.com) for others to learn from your experience. Please send a copy of your completed pages 117–118 to: The Editors, SkyLight Paths Publishing, P.O. Box 237, Woodstock, VT 05091.

We will succeed only if our books make a difference in your life. We are all *walking together, finding the way.*

Why Use a Time Capsule?

We often share hopes and aspirations with others. We also have hopes not shared, because for whatever reason they are too personal. This is often the case with our spiritual hopes and aspirations.

A time capsule offers us a way to record and focus on our hopes in a concrete way, even spiritual hopes that are very personal.

A time capsule can also function like a spiritual will. Imagine that you are gone in ten or twenty years—what *spiritual* gifts would you want to give your loved ones?

Below, write down what you feel is most important in life and who you are trying to become, as if your answers will be opened by someone you love (and you designate) ten or twenty years from now, perhaps once you are gone. Consider what your friend, spouse, brother or sister, child, godchild, grandchild, niece or nephew should learn from your spiritual experience. Seal this page—or use a separate piece of paper and seal it—in an envelope and keep it with your will, or in some other safe place where it can easily be retrieved.

If you wish to use a separate piece of paper to fill out your Ten- or Twenty-Year Time Capsule, you may photocopy these pages for that purpose.

_____-Year Time Capsule

My Spiritual Will

The following represents my "spiritual will."

Today's date: _____

I am writing here to reinforce the importance of these things for my life, and in the lives of every person who comes in contact with me. These are things I want you to know from my spiritual life. These are the hopes and gifts I have for you:

_____
NAME

_____
NAME

_____
NAME

i. *The Collected Poems of Thomas Merton* (New York: New Directions, 1977), 363.

ii. Lawrence Kushner, *Invisible Lines of Connection: Sacred Stories of the Ordinary* (Woodstock, Vt.: Jewish Lights Publishing, 1996), 100–101.

iii. Quoted in *Sierra*, a special supplement entitled "Religion and the Environment" (1999): 8.

iv. Quoted by Dorothy Day, *Dorothy Day: Selected Writings* (Maryknoll, N.Y.: Orbis, 1992), 353.

v. Moshe Mykoff and the Breslov Research Institute, *The Empty Chair: Finding Hope and Joy—Timeless Wisdom from a Hasidic Master, Rebbe Nachman of Breslov* (Woodstock, Vt.: Jewish Lights Publishing, 1994), 50.

vi. Kojiro Nakamura, trans., *Ghazali on Prayer* (Tokyo: Institute of Oriental Culture, 1973), 109.

vii. Tamar Frankiel and Judy Greenfeld, *Minding the Temple of the Soul: Balancing Body, Mind, and Spirit through Traditional Jewish Prayer, Movement, and Meditation* (Woodstock, Vt.: Jewish Lights Publishing, 1997), 15–17. Frankiel and Greenfeld are also the authors of *Entering the Temple of Dreams: Jewish Prayers, Movements, and Meditations for the End of the Day* (Woodstock, Vt.: Jewish Lights Publishing, 2000.)

viii. Lyn Klug, ed., *Soul Weavings* (Minneapolis, Minn.: Augsburg Fortress Press, 1996).

ix. Sri Krishna, The Bhagavad Gita, from *The End of Sorrow: The Bhagavad Gita for Daily Living, Vol. 1* by Eknath Easwaran (Berkeley, Calif.: Nilgiri Press, 1997), 149.

x. Paul Reps and Nyogen Senzaki, compilers, *Zen Flesh Zen Bones* (Boston: Tuttle, 1998), 38–39.

xi. George Appleton, ed., *The Oxford Book of Prayer* (New York: Oxford University Press, 1985), 14.

xii. Quoted in *Utne Reader,* "Should You Design Your Own Religion?" (August 1998): 48.

Karen Armstrong is a British historian of religion, a journalist and a former nun. Her several award-winning books include *A History of God: The 4,000-Year Quest of Judaism, Christianity and Islam; Jerusalem: One City, Three Faiths* and *Islam: A Shory History.*

Sylvia Boorstein is one of our most articulate teachers of Buddhism and mindfulness meditation. A founding teacher at Spirit Rock Meditation Center in Woodacre, California, Boorstein is also a senior teacher at the Insight Meditation Society in Barre, Massachusetts, and the author of the best-selling books *It's Easier Than You Think: The Buddhist Way to Happiness; Don't Just Do Something, Sit There* and *That's Funny, You Don't Look Buddhist.*

Frederic and Mary Ann Brussat are two of the most respected book and media reviewers working in religion and spirituality today. They regularly review for *Spirituality & Health* magazine and on www.spiritualrx.com, and are the authors of *Spiritual Literacy: Reading the Sacred in Everyday Life* and *Spiritual Rx: Prescriptions for Living a Meaningful Life.*

Rabbi David A. Cooper has studied mysticism for over 30 years. His main practice has been spiritual retreats and meditation in a number of traditions, including Sufi, Vipassana, Kabbalah and Zen. He is the award-winning author of many books, including the bestseller *God Is a Verb; Silence, Simplicity & Solitude: A Complete Guide to Spiritual Retreat at Home; Three Gates to Meditation Practice: A Personal Journey into Sufism, Buddhism, and Judaism; A Heart of Stillness: A Complete Guide to Learning the Art of Meditation* and *The Handbook of Jewish Meditation Practices: A Guide for Enriching the Sabbath and Other Days of Your Life.*

Brother Victor-Antoine d'Avila-Latourrette is a resident monk at Our Lady of the Resurrection Monastery near Millbrook, New York. He works as cook and gardener at the monastery, and is the author of several books including *Fresh from a Monastery Garden* and *Twelve Months of Monastery Soups.*

Mitch Finley is widely recognized as an expert in bringing spiritual ideas "down to earth." He is the recipient of seven Catholic Press Awards and an Excellence in Writing Award from the American Society of Journalists and Authors. His many award-winning books include *The Seeker's Guide to the Christian Story; Prayer for People Who Think Too Much: A Guide to Everyday, Anywhere Prayer from the World's Faith Traditions* and *The Joy of Being Catholic.*

Dr. Eugene Fisher is a leader in interfaith dialogue and a member of the National Conference of Catholic Bishops' Committee for Ecumenical and Interreligious Affairs. His contributions in this book are taken from a joint statement of Catholic and Jewish leaders entitled "Reflections on the Millennium." He is the author of *Faith without Prejudice: Rebuilding Christian Attitudes toward Judaism.*

Tamar Frankiel, Ph.D., and **Judy Greenfeld** are the authors of *Minding the Temple of the Soul: Balancing Body, Mind, and Spirit through Traditional Jewish Prayer, Movement, and Meditation* and *Entering the Temple of Dreams: Jewish Prayers, Movements, and Meditations for the End of the Day.* Frankiel teaches the history of religions at the University of California, Riverside, and is the author of *The Gift of Kabbalah: Discovering the Secrets of Heaven, Renewing Your Life on Earth.* Greenfeld is a certified fitness trainer and founder of Homeaerobics, Inc., a personal fitness training company in southern California.

Matthew Gilbert is widely considered to be one of our most insightful commentators on contemporary trends in religion. He is the former executive editor of *NAPRA ReView,* and author of *Take This Job & Love It: How to Find Fulfillment in Any Job You Do.*

Father Joseph F. Girzone retired from the active priesthood in 1981 and has since become a best-selling author. In 1995 he created the Joshua Foundation, an organization established to make Jesus better known around the world. His many books include the *Joshua* series and *A Portrait of Jesus.*

Rev. Theodore M. Hesburgh, csc, is the president emeritus, University of Notre Dame, having served as the school's active president from 1952 to 1987. He is widely considered one of the most respected academic leaders in the United States, has counseled 15 U.S. presidents and three popes, and is the subject of a new scholarly biography.

Rodger Kamenetz is a poet and teacher of literature, and the award-winning author of *The Jew in the Lotus: A Poet's Rediscovery of Jewish Identity in Buddhist India; Terra Infirma* and *Stalking Elijah.*

Lawrence Kushner is widely regarded as one of the most creative theologians and storytellers in America. His acclaimed books include *Honey from the Rock: An Introduction to Jewish Mysticism; The Book of Letters: A Mystical Hebrew Alphabet; The Way Into Jewish Mystical Tradition; Jewish Spirituality: A Brief Introduction for Christians; Eyes Remade for Wonder: A Lawrence Kushner Reader*, with an introduction by Thomas Moore; and, with Karen Kushner, the children's book *Because Nothing Looks Like God*. He is Rabbi-in-Residence at Hebrew Union College in New York and a guest commentator on National Public Radio's *All Things Considered*.

Patrick Marrin is one of the most respected Catholic journalists in America today. He is the editor of Celebration Publications, part of the National Catholic Reporter Publishing Co.

Katherine Paterson is one of the most decorated authors of books for children and young adults. The winner of two prestigious Newbery Awards, she is the author of numerous books including *Jip: His Story* and *Jacob Have I Loved*.

Father M. Basil Pennington, OCSO, is a monk in the Cistercian order and widely respected as one of our most profound teachers on prayer. He is the author of many award-winning books including *Lectio Divina: Renewing the Ancient Practice of Praying the Scriptures* and *A Place Apart: Monastic Prayer and Practice for Everyone*.

Sandy Eisenberg Sasso is widely recognized as an inspiring advocate for the spirituality of children. The author of many award-winning books including *God's Paintbrush; In God's Name; A Prayer for the Earth: The Story of Naamah, Noah's Wife* and *Cain & Abel: Finding the Fruits of Peace,* Sasso is rabbi of Congregation Beth-El Zedeck in Indianapolis and active in the interfaith community. She is the second woman to be ordained a rabbi (1974) and the first rabbi to become a mother.

Kathy Shaidle is one of the brightest young writers of spirituality in North America. A Canadian, she lives in Toronto and is the author of *God Rides a Yamaha: Musings on Prayer, Poetry and Pop Culture* and *Lobotomy Magnificat,* her first collection of poetry.

Dr. Bernie Siegel was one of the first innovators to awaken us to the power of alternative medicine and the spiritual side of healing. He was a practicing surgeon in New Haven, Connecticut, until he retired in 1989 and became the best-selling author of *Love, Medicine and Miracles: Lessons Learned About Self-Healing from a Surgeon's Experience with Exceptional Patients* and *Prescriptions for Living.*

Rt. Rev. Krister Stendahl is one of the most respected Christian church leaders of the second half of the 20th century. The bishop emeritus of Stockholm (Lutheran) and former dean of Harvard Divinity School, Stendahl has written many books about the New Testament and Jewish–Christian dialogue including *Paul Among Jews and Gentiles.*

Phyllis Tickle is one of the most quoted experts on religion in America today. She is contributing editor in religion to *Publishers Weekly* and the author of many books including *God-Talk in America* and *The Divine Hours* series.

Rabbi Arthur Waskow is recognized as one of the seminal thinkers of the Jewish renewal movement. A leading creator of Jewish renewal theory, practice and institutions, and a Pathfinder of ALEPH: Alliance for Jewish Renewal, Waskow is director of the Shalom Center, and author of several books including *Godwrestling—Round 2: Ancient Wisdom, Future Paths; Down-to-Earth Judaism* and *Torah of the Earth: Exploring 4,000 Years of Ecology in Jewish Thought.*

Dr. Andrew Weil is a Harvard-trained physician and our most articulate teacher of holistic medicine and healing. He is the author of the best-selling books *Spontaneous Healing: How to Discover and Enhance Your Body's Natural Ability to Maintain and Heal Itself* and *8 Weeks to Optimum Health.*

Jane Yolen is the author of more than 200 books for children and adults and the winner of many awards. These exceptional books include *Owl Moon,* winner of the Caldecott Medal, and *Milk & Honey: A Year of Jewish Holidays.*